C000263957

Around Slough

IN OLD PHOTOGRAPHS

Dear Ian,

Memories of Slough!

Thank you to you and Carol
for being the best neighbours ever!

Love from

Sandra Alex Ella
   x   x   x

Matt Ken
  x

Crown Corner, 1935. Slough developed as a medieval village at the crossroads now known as Crown Corner after the inn that stood on the south-east corner for over three hundred years. The inn, rebuilt in 1932, can be seen almost in the centre of the photograph. The High Street runs diagonally from top left to bottom right, with William Street running to the bottom left. At the centre of the crossroads is an ornate lamp-post. Opposite the Crown are buildings which once belonged to Slough Farm. In 1935 the farm, with some of the appurtenant buildings, was used as offices by Slough Urban District Council.

Around Slough

IN OLD PHOTOGRAPHS

Collected by
JUDITH AND KAREN HUNTER

Alan Sutton Publishing Limited
Phoenix Mill · Far Thrupp
Stroud · Gloucestershire

First published 1992

Copyright © Judith and Karen Hunter, 1992

BERKSHIRE BOOKS

Dedicated to the memory of Kathie Marshall who contributed so much to the Photographic Collection at Slough Museum.

British Library Cataloguing
in Publication Data

Hunter, Judith
  Around Slough in Old Photographs
  I. Title II. Hunter, Karen
  942.297

  ISBN 0-7509-0196-9

Typeset in 9/10 Sabon.
Typesetting and origination by
Alan Sutton Publishing Limited.
Printed in Great Britain by
WBC Press Ltd, Bridgend.

Fire at the old Crown Inn, 1929. The history of the inn has been traced back as far as 1618 and the building which survived until 1932 almost certainly contained seventeenth-century timbers, However, the façade shown in the photograph is Georgian, built when the Crown was Slough's most important coaching and posting inn.

Contents

Observatory House, Windsor Road. William Herschel, the town's most famous resident, came to Slough in 1786. Here he set up his 20 ft telescope and set about building his 40 ft instrument with a grant received from George III. By the time the giant telescope was completed, the name Slough had become famous throughout Europe. The house stood opposite the Granada Cinema.

High Street looking east, 1905. Notice the number of projecting ornamental gas lamps on the right hand side of the street. The building with the large clock was the Public Hall and Leopold Institute which was opened in 1887 by the Duchess of Albany, widow of Prince Leopold, Queen Victoria's youngest son. To many local people, Slough is its High Street, a place to shop and meet friends.

Introduction

During the one hundred and fifty years since photography first added a new dimension to our records of the past, Slough grew from a small but important village on the Bath Road to a densely populated industrial borough. But no photographer captured a view of the village with its coaching inns or of the early stages of Slough's development into a market town following the construction of the Great Western Railway line; the earliest known photographs date from the last quarter of the nineteenth century, by which time a stretch of the Bath Road had changed its name and became the town's High Street.

Slough remained a small country town for about eighty years, growing relatively slowly but soon absorbing the village of Upton, once the main settlement in the parish of Upton cum Chalvey. Until this century, Chalvey and the other areas which today make up the suburbs were still villages, separated from Slough by farmland, nursery gardens and brickfields.

In 1918 the War Office established a motor repair depot on land just to the west of Slough in the parish of Farnham Royal. The enterprise was a disaster, but its sale to a group of businessmen after the end of the war heralded the beginning of a new chapter in the history of Slough. The motor depot became Slough Trading Estate and then Slough Estates, the first such industrial organization in the country. It brought industry, employment and people to Slough in great numbers, and during the depression years of the 1930s Slough was one of the few areas in the country where there were still jobs to be found. Farmland began to disappear under new housing estates and factory sites. By 1931 Slough's population was over 33,000, a 65 per cent increase in ten years, and its civic boundaries had been extended to take in large parts of the parishes of Burnham, Farnham Royal, Stoke Poges and Langley. In 1938 Slough Urban District was elevated to the status of a borough.

For the authors, 1938 is a lifetime away, and much has happened to Slough since that date. New industrial and residential areas and redevelopment schemes have continued to change the appearance of the town, so much so that photographs of the 1960s and 1970s are already of historical value. Buildings, public and private, have been built and demolished, and many have changed their use. But a town is so much more than its buildings and streets, and it is the photographs of people that catch our imagination and provide a feel for the past, be they of important people and public events or of everyday scenes which portray facets of Slough's past.

Increasingly over the past fifty years, Slough has become a very cosmopolitan town, its residents coming from all over the world. The process began when Slough first became a town; the community then included people from almost every county in the country and a few from overseas. During the last fifty years people have migrated to Slough in great numbers from other parts of the British Isles and from many areas of the world, in particular Poland, Italy, the West Indies, India, Pakistan, South Asia and East Africa. Today there are more than thirty ethnic minority organizations representing the cultural, educational and social interests of their members.

In recent years Slough Library and Slough Museum have built up good collections of old and new photographs of which we were able to make great use in this book. But they represent only a fraction of the photographs which exist in private hands, in family albums and private collections. It was our privilege and pleasure to be allowed to select photographs from several private collections and to be loaned individual photographs by a great number of other people. *Slough Observer* also gave us access to its files of negatives.

With so many photographs to choose from, it might be thought easy to decide which to select. But decisions about themes soon revealed the gaps and, try as we might, we failed to find photographs to cover some areas of the town and periods and aspects of the town's history. In spite of these difficulties, we hope we have succeeded in choosing a great diversity of photographs. We first chose those which were visually pleasing, or immediately caught our interest, and then widened our selection to give a more balanced view of the different parts of the town and the neighbouring parishes, and of some of the events which have shaped its history. We have included several taken in the 1960s, '70s and even '80s, to jog the memories of those who are relative newcomers to the town. To know something of the history of a town is one way of becoming part of it.

SECTION ONE
Central Slough

The Red Lion was the second most important inn in Slough; it stood on the corner of the High Street on a site now occupied by the Prudential building. It became a coaching and posting inn but, unlike the Crown Inn, it did not become a hotel after the railway had diminished its coaching trade.

The White Hart and Foresters Arms. The White Hart was a stage coach inn and a receiving house for the Royal Mail. The adjacent Foresters Arms was a mere beer shop. Both were demolished to make way for the new library and office development in the 1970s.

Public Library, *c.* 1940. This building was Slough's first purpose-built library. Today it is a day centre for the elderly. This was the site of Slough Farm and where, in the late nineteenth century, a house known as The Cedars was built.

The new library was opened in November 1974. It is officially known as the Robert Taylor Library after Alderman Robert Taylor who was the first honorary librarian in Slough and who gave a lifetime of work to provide a library service for the town.

The Black Boy, *c.* 1906. The Black Boy stood more or less opposite the present library. Its history can be traced back to the seventeenth century and it would appear that the original building survived until the pub was closed about 1910. Notice the poster urging residents to vote for Cripps on the end wall and the lack of a pictorial inn sign.

Royal visitors. Crowds lined Windsor Road and the High Street for the visit to Slough of HM King Edward VII and HM The King of Spain, probably in 1907.

Observatory House, Windsor Road. When William Herschel lived in Observatory House it stood on the southern edge of the town as shown in this early photograph of the house.

The Herschel family in the garden of Observatory House in the 1920s. At this date it was the home of Col. John Herschel. The last member of the Herschel family to live there was Miss Katherine Herschel. The house was demolished in 1960 in spite of protests by local residents.

The Granada Cinema in Windsor Road photographed only a few weeks after it was opened in 1938.

Slough Picture Hall in Windsor Road was opened in 1910 by Henry George Wilson in the grounds of the Crown Inn. It was open from 6.30 p.m. to 10.30 p.m. with a 3 o'clock matinée on Saturdays. Seats cost 3d and 6d.

Slough Scout Group about 1910. The girls must also have been Scouts since the first Girl Guide Company in Slough was not formed until 1915.

In the Second World War Slough, like every other town, played its part in the war effort. Here the mayor, Aubrey Ward, is inspecting a display in the Granada Cinema in 1942 to encourage people to conserve fuel.

Wings for Victory, 1943. An impressive array of VIPs wait in the Adelphi forecourt for the opening ceremony. In the back row are Lord Chatfield, Admiral of the Fleet, Admiral Furstner of the Netherlands Navy and Air Marshal Lywood. In the front row are the mayoress of Slough, Mrs Aubrey Ward, other local dignitaries and the US ambassador, Vincent Massey.

Second World War shortages. Slough had a 'Salvage Kid' to encourage locals to sift through their rubbish to see what could be recycled. Fifty years later recycling has again become an important issue.

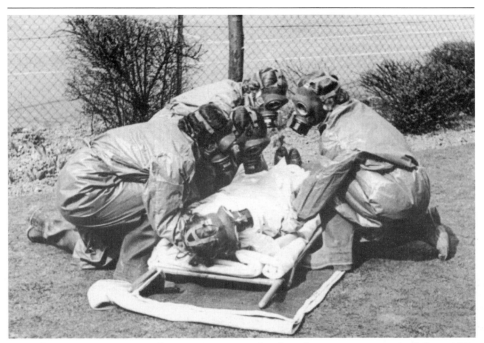

Even the patient was required to wear a gas mask when these women practised first aid in 1939.

The Decontamination Squad of the St John Ambulance Brigade pose outside the Slough and Langley Laundry van which they used during the Second World War.

High Street looking west, *c.* 1905. The large building on the right is the post office which was built in 1893; it was demolished eighty years later to make way for the Queensmere. The building in the middle distance with the distinctive clock is the Public Hall and Leopold Institute.

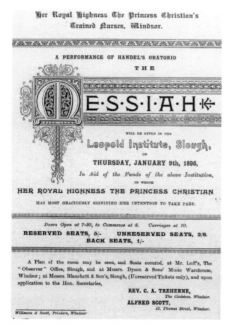

Her Royal Highness The Princess Christian's
Trained Nurses, Windsor.

A PERFORMANCE OF HANDEL'S ORATORIO

THE

M·E·S·S·I·A·H

WILL BE GIVEN IN THE

Leopold Institute, Slough,

ON

THURSDAY, JANUARY 9th, 1896,

In Aid of the Funds of the above Institution,

IN WHICH

HER ROYAL HIGHNESS THE PRINCESS CHRISTIAN

HAS MOST GRACIOUSLY SIGNIFIED HER INTENTION TO TAKE PART.

Doors Open at 7-30, to Commence at 8.   Carriages at 10.

**RESERVED SEATS, 5/-   UNRESERVED SEATS, 2/6.
BACK SEATS, 1/-**

A Plan of the room may be seen, and Seats secured, at Mr. Luff's, The "Observer" Office, Slough, and at Messrs. Dyson & Sons' Music Warehouse, Windsor; at Messrs. Blanchett & Son's, Slough, (Unreserved Tickets only), and upon application to the Hon. Secretaries.

REV. C. A. TREHERNE,
The Cloisters, Windsor.

ALFRED SCOTT,
13, Thames Street, Windsor.

Willmore & Scott, Printers, Windsor

Two programmes of events at the Public Hall, 1905 (left) and 1890 (opposite).

Slough Choral Society.

SECOND SEASON.

—o—

PROGRAMME

OF THE

FIRST CONCERT

WHICH WILL BE GIVEN IN

THE SLOUGH PUBLIC HALL,

ON

Thursday Evening, February 6th, 1890.

THE SACRED CANTATA,

"The Holy City,"

(GAUL),

WILL BE PERFORMED

WITH ORCHESTRAL ACCOMPANIMENT.

SOLOISTS :

MISS JULIA MARK,
MISS ELLA CLEUGHE.
REV. WALTER MARSHALL.   MR. G. STUBBS.

Leader of the Orchestra :—   *Pianoforte :—*
MR. H. W. HUNT, Mus. Bac.   MISS HOBLEY.

Organ :—   *Conductor :—*
MR. H. S. STANBROOK.   MR. W. T. BLANCHETT.

TICKETS.

Reserved Seats (numbered) 3/-   Front Seats 2/-
Other Seats (number limited) 1/-.

Doors Open at 8 p.m. ; Commence at 8.30.   Carriages at 10.

Tickets may be obtained, and a Plan of the Hall seen at Mr. C.
Luff's, High Street, Slough.

Slough High Street. The Belisha crossing dates the photograph as post-1950. None of the buildings (or their façades) survive today and few shops now have awnings, but Milwards still have a shop in the High Street.

The Rose and Crown is one of the few public houses still to be found in the High Street. Bruce and Lumb's remain in Burlington Road and there is still a café next to the Rose and Crown.

A busy scene in the High Street looking west. Notice the horse-drawn cart and the perambulator.

The east end of the High Street, c. 1960. The large building is the David Greig house, erected in 1932; to the left is Grove Parade. Was the shop on the right Slough's first supermarket?

Thomas Page's ironmongers shop had a prominent site in the High Street opposite
Mackenzie Street early this century. Shopkeepers often took great pride in the arrange-
ment of their wares.

This view of the High Street in 1896 is one of the earliest known; Richard Abraham's grocery shop was established at No. 80 some ten years earlier and remained at the same site until at least the mid-1920s. However, it is difficult to reconcile the shop fronts in this picture with those of later photographs.

Renacre's ironmongers shop at No. 4 Windsor Road was established sometime before 1915; it did not close until the 1980s and the name still evokes fond memories in tradesmen and DIY householders.

A great fire at Slough. On 1 January 1903 a fire totally destroyed the shop of Butler and Bowden, 'universal providers', and badly damaged the shop of Mr Hucker, painter and decorator. The newspaper reported that Slough Fire Brigade spent six and a half hours dealing with the fire and used 91,000 gallons of water.

Parades took place most years between the wars. They were joyful occasions, an opportunity for publicity for the shops taking part but also for collecting money for charity. In 1938 Slough Co-op had its own carnival.

A church parade in 1908 was a colourful occasion and a highlight of the year.

The Methodist Central Hall was opened in 1932 by HRH The Duchess of York (now the Queen Mother). Crowds waited to watch and the traffic was diverted to the side streets. The photograph shows heads bowed during a moment of prayer. The hall, which could seat a thousand people, stood at the corner of the Grove and the High Street. It was demolished in 1966.

St Andrew's church in the Grove replaced the Central Hall, and it was to have been opened by Her Majesty The Queen Mother. Unfortunately she was taken seriously ill and could not do so. However, a year later she attended a morning service, toured the building and talked to the Revd Howard Ford and members of the congregation.

William Street in the 1930s. Many people remember Foster Brothers, but how many recall the telephone kiosk in the middle of the road?

W. Allen's shoe repairs shop in William Street. Even the humblest shops celebrated George VI's coronation with at least some decorations!

William Street in the 1950s. In the twenty years which separates this view from the one opposite it is the differences in traffic and road markings, rather than buildings, which mark the passage of time. But on the right hand side the Prudential building has replaced the Red Lion Inn and other premises.

High Street from Mackenzie Street, *c.* 1928. This part of the High Street has not been redeveloped but the ornate lamp-post, with its sign pointing the way to the station, has long since been removed; today it is the site of the Queensmere fountains. Headington's shop was the retail outlet for Cippenham Court Farm and many people remember its window display with diamond patterns made with different coloured seeds. The National Westminster Bank (successor to the National Provincial) still own the bank building shown, but has moved next door.

Mackenzie Street originally led from the High Street to Station Approach; today it is one of the entrances into the Queensmere.

Boys Brigade brass band are seen marching into the Licensed Victuallers' School, Mackenzie Street, about 1950. The school was built on the site of the original Royal Hotel; today it has been replaced by Tesco's supermarket. The Dodds Repositories in the background belonged to G.E. Dodd & Son, coal merchants and removals.

The Minister of Transport, Harold Watkinson, visited Slough during 1956 when the town was the subject of a pedestrian crossing experiment. Here he is seen crossing the road after he had officially switched on the push-button controlled lights.

The first Belisha pedestrian crossing in Slough, 1950. This was replaced by the zebra crossing and then the controlled light crossing in 1956. There is still a pedestrian crossing here at the west end of the High Street.

The Prince of Wales. The present public house stands on the same site as the original beer house. When the pub was first opened in 1842 it was outside the town.

Funeral procession of 'Mr and Mrs Harbert's three dear little children', Marjorie, Doris and Beatrice, who were suffocated in the worst fire known in Slough, according to the newspaper report of March 1905.

Charter celebrations. The mayor, E. Bowyer, is planting a tree in Lascelles playing fields during the Borough Charter celebrations of 1938.

Slough Borough Council. In this official photograph taken in May 1940, members of the town's first Borough Council are seen outside the newly built Town Hall.

A royal proclamation, Slough, 1950. For centuries the Crown has issued orders by royal proclamations but few photographs capture the informal action of the mayor pinning a proclamation dissolving Parliament on a notice board. The mayor, John Taylor, is accompanied by the deputy town clerk, George Moxham.

SECTION TWO
Slough's Villages

Upton was the first of the villages within modern Slough to be absorbed by the growing town. By the early nineteenth century its Norman church was in a poor state of repair, it was replaced as the parish church in 1836 by the newly built St Mary's at Slough. The brickwork of the parish pound can be seen on the left.

Floods in Datchet Road near the Myrke, 1903. Upton was well named for the village was built above the Thames flood plain. The Myrke (an ancient word meaning boundary) was on the low ground. The vehicle is thought to have been carrying passengers.

The Mere was built in 1887 by George Bentley, editor of the *Temple Bar Magazine*. Today the Mere is home to the National Foundation for Educational Research.

LA DYNASTIE DES BENTLEY

| Edward | Samuel | Richard senior | George | Richard junior |

The Bentley family. This print of five members of the family is taken from a biography, *Les Grands Editeurs Anglais*, printed in 1886. The first Richard Bentley was Charles Dickens's publisher. It was his son, George, who built the Mere. George's son, Richard Bentley, author and publisher, lived at the Mere until 1936.

One of the three lodge gates of Upton Park. This gate at Arbour Hill was demolished in the 1980s. The park originally contained twenty-nine superior houses and spacious grounds complete with an ornamental lake; it was built in 1841 by James Bedborough of Windsor.

The Fair View convalescent home in Upton Road was established sometime before 1920 for patients from the Children's Hospital at Paddington Green in London. It took about twenty children from poor families.

Go-karts for Upton Court playing fields. In March 1962 the mayor, Noel Eschele, the chairman of the road safety committee, Frank Warwick, councillor Alan Simpson, and the parks superintendent, Leslie Scrase, tested the new go-karts before the decision was made to build a go-kart track.

Chalvey Road, 1913. The building which houses the Empire Cinema was built as a Congregational chapel in 1835; it was taken over by the Primitive Methodists some twenty years later. The boards outside the newsagents proclaim 'Mrs Pankhurst decides to starve' and 'Sir Percy Scott exposed'.

Church Street, Chalvey. Floods were a frequent feature of life in Chalvey. This one of 1918 was by no means as memorable as those of 1894 and 1947 when many houses were inundated.

Chalvey High Street early this century. Once the busy heart of Chalvey village, today there are no shops and none of the buildings shown in the photograph still exist.

The Crescent around the turn of the century. The photograph shows how little has changed since the houses were built – except for the parked cars – but note the evidence of horse traffic! The inhabitants of a hundred years ago could scarcely have imagined the traffic situation which has made a one-way system necessary.

Tuns Lane crossroads. It is difficult to recognize this junction as the site of the Chalvey roundabout. To the left is Tuns Lane, now the dual carriageway leading to the Three Tuns public house; to the right is Cippenham Lane.

Chalvey Grove was once a curving track running round the edge of a large common known as Chalvey Green and Chalvey Grove. The common itself disappeared nearly two hundred years ago, but as late as 1975 when this photograph was taken not all the farm-land had been lost to housing.

The new Chalvey Dairy. Its opening was celebrated in 1938. A few years later, when rationing was introduced during the war, 21,500 people registered there.

W. Napper, dairyman of Chalvey. In the early years of this century housewives brought out their jugs to be filled from the measures which are hanging on the side of his handcart.

The Cape of Good Hope was a small beer house in Chalvey Grove. In the 1930s Mr Holdway, the licensee, achieved local fame by his discovery of the long lost Chalvey Stab Monk, a plaster cast of a monkey which had become part of Chalvey's folklore.

The Cross Keys, first licensed in 1824, is the oldest surviving public house in Chalvey. It was rebuilt about 1930 at a time when breweries were very proud of their 'improved' houses. The cross keys are a sign of St Peter and so presumably the inn sign refers to the nearby church of St Peter, but if so the pub has been renamed for the church was not built until some thirty-five years after the pub was first opened.

Chalvey railway bridge. The original bridge was demolished in the 1930s to allow the road to be widened. Chalvey also lost its small station, Chalvey Halt, built in 1929.

The new bridge looks much the same today although the crossroads beneath is now a busy road junction.

Chalvey National School: class 3B. As in most village schools, girls and boys were taught separately from about the age of seven.

Chalvey National infants class, *c*. 1920.

Chalvey Girl Guides and Brownies, 1919.

Garden party at the Old Rectory at Chalvey. It is not known when or why Princess Helena, daughter of Queen Victoria, and her own daughter Princess Marie Louise were invited to this particular garden party, but Princess Helena was a renowned social worker and genuinely cared about the conditions of the poor.

Salt Hill Park was the first recreation ground to be provided for Slough residents. It was opened in 1907 and included the cottage for the park superintendent which can be seen in the distance. The park was founded through the generosity of James Elliman who provided the land, the buildings and landscaping, and presented the park to the people of Slough. He also gave £10,000 to be invested for its upkeep.

Salt Hill Park: an idyllic view of the Chalvey Brook flowing through the park.

The Barn was part of James Elliman's original concept for the park; a place where visitors could obtain a welcome cup of tea. In the early 1970s the Barn was used for weekend gatherings by the Sikh community. Today it is a Tandoori restaurant.

Opening of Slough Museum, 1986. The first curator, Karen Hull, is sitting with John Watts, MP, in a 1930s room in the museum. Leeds Cottage, which houses the main part of the museum, was built about 1930.

The mayor, Cyril Gibbs, is seen 'on museum opening day', polishing his Citroen which was assembled in Slough.

Cippenham village centre, *c.* 1920. Today the three public houses, the war memorial and nearby village pond are part of suburban Slough.

Mr Stone's delivery van in the 1930s. It was probably a recent addition to the business.

Butchers shop. Mr E. Stone and his two delivery boys are posing outside the shop on the Bath Road in the early 1930s.

The nurses hostel in Cippenham Lane was built in 1902 for the Eton Rural District to deal with infectious diseases, such as diptheria, which could be fatal. It served Cippenham and Slough. It was closed about 1948 with the introduction of the National Health Service. It then became a nurses hostel.

An isolation hospital was built somewhere north of the railway line. It is thought to have been demolished in 1918 to make way for the War Office Motor Transport Depot.

Open Day at the sewage works, Wood Lane in the mid-1970s soon after Thames Water
Authority took over from Slough Borough Council.

Cippenham Court Farm was once the desmene farm of the lord of the manor. Although some of the buildings still exist, it ceased to be a farm about 1980. The stables on the right have been converted to the Long Barn public house. The grassy area, seen in this 1970s photograph, was once the farm midden; today it is the pub terrace and car park.

The cart horse stable, Cippenham Court Farm, *c.* 1924. Today this is the bar in the Long Barn public house.

Hoeing at Cippenham Court Farm. In 1910 most farm work still involved much hard and back-breaking labour. This is one of a series of photographs taken at this date showing the work on the farm.

Lewen's Farm milk cart, 1924. The name is found in fifteenth-century documents and today as a street name. The farm was still being worked in the 1960s. Notice that the milk round appears to be a joint enterprise with E. Neville of William Street.

SLOUGH & DISTRICT CO-OPERATIVE SOCIETY L^{TD}

PROVISIONS   GROCERY

The new Co-op shop at Cippenham. This purpose-built shop replaced a wooden hut which had been converted into a shop. Although the shop ceased to be used by the Co-op many years ago, the building was only recently demolished.

Slough High School, Twinches Lane. Built in 1936 as the first school in Slough to offer grammar school education for girls only, it was demolished in 1986 only months before its fiftieth anniversary.

Horsemoor Green, Langley. Today the road is known as Langley High Street, but until the early nineteenth century the village houses were built around a green and the present road was merely a track across it.

High Street, Langley. Almost the same view as the previous photograph, this one, taken at a later date, shows Marish Court with its distinctive roof line. Note the change of brewers supplying the Crown public house. The pub was rebuilt and renamed the Tiara; today it is called the Arkle.

Langley village hall, *c*. 1916. The hall was built in 1889 at Horsemoor Green and used for religious and social purposes.

The pond, Langley. This picturesque view could once be seen as one travelled from Langley Road to the Harrow public house.

St Bernard's Convent. Aldin House, as it was originally known, was built for Baroness Burdett-Coutts, a member of the banking family, though she never lived there. For fourteen years from 1869 it was St Michael's School. In 1897 it was bought by the Bernardines and given its present name.

The grand staircase in St Bernard's Convent.

SLOUGH

ST. BERNARD'S CONVENT SCHOOL

Boarding and Day School for Girls

Recognised for Efficiency by the Board of Education
Excellent Results in Examinations and Games

For Prospectus apply to the HEAD MISTRESS

Advertisement for the two schools belonging to the convent. See page 96 for a photograph of St Joseph's.

St Mary's church, Langley is one of the two oldest churches in the Borough. This postcard also shows the old vicarage which the vicar in 1866 found far too small for his family and an 'unfit abode' for a married clergyman because of its proximity to the brickfields.

Green Drive, Langley. It has long been believed that this drive was created for Sarah, Duchess of Marlborough, as a convenient short cut on her journey from Windsor to Langley Park. It might even be true!

Mr Percy Beckett became one of the well-known and well-loved characters of Langley when he dressed in his shepherd's smock and collected for charity at numerous local events.

Wexham Park Mansion. The house built between 1861 and 1864 for Joseph Grote stood in some forty acres of parkland. It was later demolished to make way for Wexham Park Hospital.

Wexham Park Hospital was built in 1966 to cater for the increased population of Slough and the neighbourhood. It took over from Upton Hospital as the main hospital for the town.

The first patients being received at the hospital.

The reception area, photographed in 1966, looks very much as it does today, but it will shortly be altered partly to comply with stricter fire regulations.

Wexham village and post office, 1930s. At his date Wexham was a very small parish with no public house or other shops. This building has been used as a post office for many years.

Miss Midge in pony and trap belonging to Green's Dairy outside the post office.

SECTION THREE

Northern Slough

Stoke Road mission chapel was built in 1885 to serve the growing population in this part of Slough. The money was given by Mr Algernon Gilliat, a patient of Dr Buee who lived in The Cedars, William Street from about 1860. The chapel was a landmark and affectionately known as the 'tin tabernacle'.

Where it all began. In one of these cottages in Stoke Gardens religious meetings were held by Kate Buee, the doctor's daughter. Her work inspired Mr Gilliat to build the chapel.

Stoke Road at the turn of the century. The spire in the distance is that of the mission chapel. In 1905 Mr Gilliat provided the money for a new church – St Paul's in Stoke Road – to replace the old mission chapel.

St Paul's Sunday School outing, 1912. Before the Second World War Burnham Beeches was the destination of many Sunday School outings. Tradesmen's carts were scrubbed for the occasion and the day brought the excitement of the journey, a picnic and organized games.

This aerial photograph of Manor Park in the early 1930s shows three phases in its development. The road leading from the bottom of the map into the centre is Essex Avenue/Villiers Road; on either side of the latter are the streets of the first phase. The curving road on the left is Northern Road, the main road of the second phase. In the middle distance are the houses and building land for the third phase. St John's church has not yet been built.

MANOR PARK CONSTRUCTION CO.
LIMITED

Phone 1400

STOKE POGES LANE, SLOUGH, BUCKS

Land Owners and
Developers
And Builders of

1530 HOUSES FOR SLOUGH COUNCIL
550 PRIVATE HOUSES. Numerous SHOPS
AMBASSADOR CINEMA, FARNHAM ROAD

THE COMPANY'S LATEST UNDERTAKING

NEW COMMODORE CINEMA, CIPPENHAM

BALL ROOM
CAFE
SHOPS

SEATING
CAPACITY
1500

Advertisement of the Manor Park Construction Company.

Floods at Manor Park Estate in 1947.

Residents of Waterbeach Road celebrated the end of hostilities in Europe on VE Day, 1945, with a street party.

Church choir procession marching through Slough Trading Estate in 1962.

Slough's first council houses were built in 1919, only a year after the Housing Act which encouraged local councils to build working class 'homes for heroes', the First World War soldiers.

The Farnham Road of the 1930s had not yet become one long shopping parade although dwelling houses were already being converted to shops. The George was opened in 1921, a substantial public house, built to cater for the workers and residents of this part of the town next to Slough Trading Estate.

Slough Social Centre was opened in 1937; it was the first community centre of its kind in this country. It was founded to provide recreational activities of all kinds beneficial to the health and well being of its members.

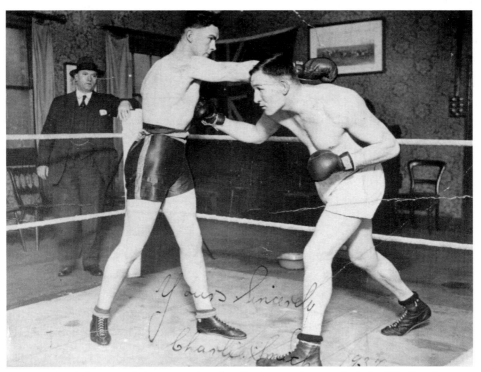

Boxing was only one of the recreational activities – others included billiards, dancing, darts, debates, elocution lessons, football, needlework, swimming and table tennis.

The first meeting place of the Britwell Residents Association was the old canteen used by the workers who built the Britwell Estate in the mid-1950s.

The opening of the new Britwell Community Centre in 1966.

The Britwell Boys' Club was opened in 1962 by the Lord Lieutenant of Buckinghamshire, Sir Henry Floyd. It was the first purpose-built boy's club in the county and at its opening 110 boys were members.

Britwell's adventure playground was constructed in 1962 to answer the urgent need for safe places for children to play.

The Mill House, Hay Mill from a painting by J. Herbert Small, 1895. The mill is thought to have been the successor to the 'Ay Mill' which belonged to Burnham Abbey in the thirteenth century.

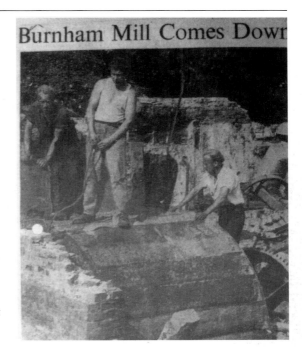

Burnham Mill Comes Down

The demolition of the Hay Mill, Windsor Lane, took place in 1960 to make way for a petrol station. In the 1920s farmers and corn merchants kept the miller busy but by the late 1940s there was little work for the mill.

Baylis House was built about 1690 for Dr Gregory Hascard, Dean of Windsor. The third storey is an eighteenth-century addition which was gutted by a fire in 1954 and subsequently removed during restoration of the house.

Baylis swimming pool. Notice the dolphin on top of the gate; it commemorated the Godolphin family who bought Baylis House in 1718 and were important local land-owners until 1920. The swimming pool was built during the period when the house was a hotel, 1923–36.

SECTION FOUR

Road and Rail

The Reading and London coach travelling along the Bath Road, *c.* 1820. It appears to have been more important for the artist to include Windsor Castle and Eton College than portray an accurate scene; no photographer could have captured such a view!

Coach and four outside the Crown Inn, 1892. By this date the Crown had long since become a hotel and stage coaches had ceased to operate along the Bath Road. This coach was being used for the Liberal Party's election campaign.

Motorcycle and sidecar passing through Salt Hill, *c.* 1920. Even though the car had been invented some thirty years before, the motor era had hardly begun and the motorcyclist apparently felt there was no necessity to keep to the left hand side of the road.

An AA patrolman at Langley Road junction. AA 'scouts' were patrolling this stretch of the road during the weekends as early as 1909, their military style uniform remaining unchanged for about forty years. In the background is St Joseph's School.

Patrolled Roads.

Alphabetically arranged in order of Routes and Districts.

BATH ROAD.—*SLOUGH.*

Hounslow - Twyford	*Inspector.*
Slough - Twyford	*Full week.*
Maidenhead - Twyford	,,
Slough - Colnbrook	,,
Hounslow - Colnbrook	*Week end.*
Slough - Colnbrook	,,
Slough, Point Duty	,,
Maidenhead - Twyford	,,
Maidenhead - Slough	,,

The first edition of the AA Handbook, 1909.

Fullbrook's filling station and garage, Slough High Street, 1928. Fullbrook's was one of the first engineering firms in Slough to offer garage facilities and to operate a filling station.

ENGLAND—Continued.

Town or Village.	Agent's Name.	Postal Address.	Tel. Address.	Tel. No.	Open Night	Open Sun	Garage Accom.	Repairing Facilities.	* Tyres Stocked.	Nearest Main Road.	† Mil'g London
AYLESBURY	A. G. Bowker	23, High-st	Bowker	PO 43	At call	At call	6	Full, Pit Vulcanizer	D	—	40¾
BEACONS-FIELD	Beaconsfield Garage	High-st	Garage Beaconsf'ld	16	Yes	Break down only	12	Full, Vulcanizer	D, Ga.	London—Oxford	23¼
BUCKINGHAM	Phillips &Son	Buckingham	Phillips Buckingh'm	21 Buckingham	No	If re-quir'd	6	Running	Cl, D	London—Banbury	55½
CHESHAM	W. Foster	134, High-st	—	PO 21	Yes	Yes	12	General	D	High-st, Chesham	29
FENNY STRATFORD	Geo. Thos. Gazeley	58, High-st	Gazeley, Fenny-Stratford	—	At call	At call	Good	Full, Vulcanizer	D, C.	London—Coventry	45¾
GREAT MISSENDEN	C. J. King	High-st	King	—	At call	No.	1	Ordinary, No Batt.	—	London—Birmingham	31
HIGH WYCOMBE	Davenport, Vernon & Co. Ltd.	HighWycombe	D. Vernon	19	At call	At call	5	General	D, Cl.	London—Oxford	29
MARLOW	Chas. Drye	46, High-st	Drye	59	At call	Yes	6	General, Vulcanizer	M, C, Cl	Bath Road	30¾
SLOUGH	J. Fullbrook & Co.	Slough	Fullbrook	Nat 2G	Yes	Yes	—	General, Vulcanizer	M	Bath Road	20½
STONY STRATFORD	A. J. Negus & Co.	25, High-st	Negus	20	No	Yes	6-7 (100)	General	None	London Road	52¾
WADDESDON	D. Evans	High Street	Evans	—	No	Yes	—	General	D	London Road	44½
WENDOVER	E. J. Sharp	High-street	Sharp	—	No	At call	None	None	None	Aylesbury—London	35¾

The first edition of the AA Handbook, 1909.

The Bath Road at Salt Hill early this century. The terrible state of the road, rutted and dusty, could make driving an unpleasant experience. Parts of the Bath Road were tarmac-adamized in 1913.

Council workers repairing the Bath Road near the Trading Estate in 1929.

The Olympic torch being carried along the Bath Road in 1948. The torch was made at the High Duty Alloy factory in Buckingham Avenue.

These runners may well be taking part in the 1908 Olympic marathon which started from Windsor Castle, the route passing the Crown Inn and along Slough High Street. The photograph, however, has not been positively identified; there were also annual races which may have used the High Street.

The Bath Road at Langley. The motor car has brought about the transformation of the Bath Road. The modern road with its wide vista bears no resemblance to the narrow road of the early twentieth century.

The Rosery tea gardens on the Bath Road near Colnbrook were a welcome stopping place for cyclists. R. White's lemonade is still a good thirst-quencher.

Bath Road, Slough Trading Estate, *c*. 1958. The art deco façade of these factories and the tree-lined verges made this stretch of the Bath Road an attractive subject for a postcard.

Aldermaston marchers in Slough High Street, April 1962. It was the biggest 'Ban the Bomb' march since the marches began five years before. It was led by Canon John Collins, chairman of the Campaign for Nuclear Disarmament, and actively supported by Slough's MP, Fenner Brockway.

Aldermaston marchers at Everitt's Corner, Cippenham where it was joined by the Slough contingent. Nearly fifteen thousand wet and bedraggled marchers squelched their way through Slough, with some ten thousand of them being accommodated overnight in sixteen local schools. Those that slept at Wexham Court School cleaned and polished the hall before they left so that it could be used for a Sunday School gathering that morning.

Aerial photograph showing the High Street and Wellington Street in 1974, soon after the development of Wellington Street as the 'by-pass'. For centuries Slough was important because of its position on the Bath Road; travellers and the coaching and carrying trades played a large part in the prosperity of the community. In recent decades all this has changed and through-traffic no longer passes along the High Street.

Slough railway station and Royal Hotel, *c.* 1845. This first station, built some three years after the railway line, was a very inconvenient design. The platforms for both the up and down lines were on the south side of the track. The 'magnificent' Royal Hotel was owned by the GWR. The hotel was closed when it lost much of its business following the opening of the branch line to Windsor.

The Royal Hotel advertisement, *c.* 1890. After the original hotel was closed the subsidiary buildings on the opposite side of Mackenzie Street were converted to a much less pretentious Royal Hotel. However, it is unlikely that it was ever used by stage coach travellers!

Slough railway station, *c.* 1911. The station, the second at Slough, was built in 1882. Taxis still wait in the forecourt, but no longer can you catch a Great Western omnibus to take you to Burnham Beeches, Farnham Common or Beaconsfield, or order a horse cab to take you to your hotel.

The Royal Hotel and GWR station early this century. The archway into the hotel yard, a familiar landmark until very recently, advertises accommodation for landaus, victorias, broughams and brakes, as well as a garage for the use of guests' cars.

The Milnes Daimler 20 hp Jersey car outside Slough station, 1904. These vehicles were mainly hired for summer outings.

Slough station looking more or less as it does today. The building in the background is the original Royal Hotel, reconstructed to serve as an orphanage: the British Orphan Asylum, 1863–1920, the Licensed Victuallers' Orphanage, 1920–38. In 1938 the building was replaced by the Licensed Victuallers' School.

The first motorized public transport service from Slough station was introduced in 1904. There were two routes taken by motor buses travelling to Beaconsfield, one via Salt Hill and Farnham Royal, the other via Stoke Poges. This photograph shows the bus passing through Dorney Bottom.

Railway banner. This is one of two designs for the banner of the Slough branch of the union depicted on early twentieth-century postcards.

The royal funeral train (engine *King Edward*) of Edward VII, 1910, running on the wrong line between Slough and Windsor because of a mishap to an engine at Slough.

The royal train, *Windsor Castle*, at Slough in 1952 for the funeral of George VI.

The coaches of the Pembroke Express were overturned when it was derailed on the stretch of line west of Horlicks on 1 May 1959. It was travelling at a speed of 70 m.p.h. but the speedy action of a local signalman in stopping the train behind prevented a disaster and only four people were slightly injured.

Industrial Slough

Elliman's factory, Chandos Street. Elliman's Embrocation – for horses and humans – was the first commercial product to give Slough national importance in the 1850s. The business remained with the Elliman family until 1961 when it was taken over by Horlicks. The factory was demolished when Queensmere was developed.

An Elliman's employee concentrates on filling the bottles with embrocation.

VICTORIA HOUSE.

J. ELLIMAN,

LINEN AND WOOLLEN DRAPER,

SILK MERCER, HOSIER, AND HABERDASHER,

NEXT TO THE POST OFFICE,

BUCKINGHAM PLACE, SLOUGH.

FUNERALS FURNISHED.

Family Mourning.

AGENT FOR THE PATENT FUNERAL CARRIAGE.

11

Advertisement, 1846. The year before James Elliman put his embrocation on the market he advertised his High Street shop in Hunt's *Royal Directory*.

Horlicks factory. The very distinctive architecture of the Horlicks factory in Stoke Poges Lane has been a feature of Slough's landscape since 1907.

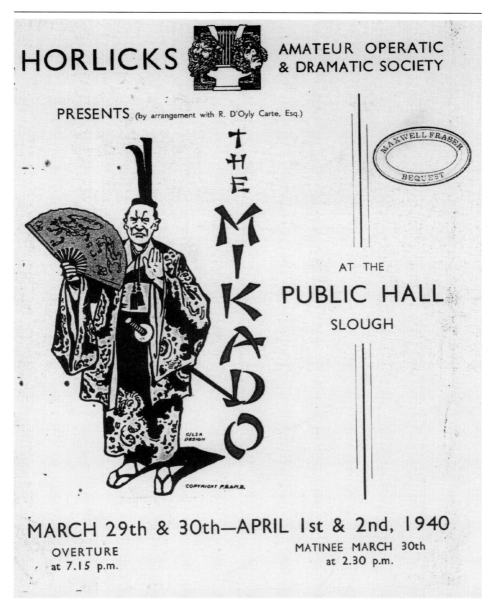

Horlicks Amateur Operatic and Dramatic Society's programme, 1940. This programme is part of the Maxwell Fraser collection in Slough library.

The Dump: the War Office Motor Repair Depot. Mud, muddle and motorized vehicles in all states of repair were responsible for the popular nickname for the War Office Depot. The depot and all the plant and vehicles were sold in 1920 to become the Slough Trading Estate.

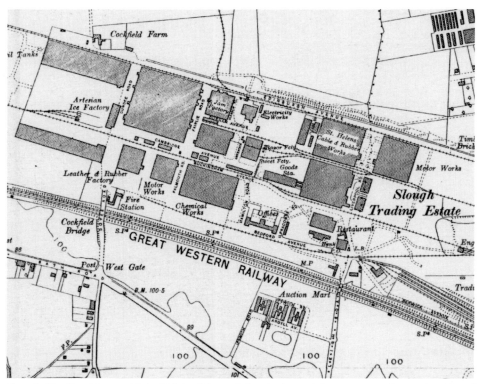

Slough Trading Estate. This 1926 edition of the Ordnance Survey map shows the site of the auction mart where hundreds of war vehicles were sold at the monthly auctions. This phase in the Estate's history ended in 1924.

Slough Estates Ltd, late 1920s. The Trading Estate was renamed in 1926 by which date the company had changed from one selling vehicles to one leasing factory space.

Art deco architecture in the 1930s. The façade of the Hanovia factory, like many others facing the main roads, was built in the architectural style of the day.

Vita-Tex factory: a view of the pressing room. Compare the building with the photograph on the page opposite.

Functional factory units. The factories were all owned by Slough Estates Ltd, not by the firms occupying them. A few of these 1920s and 1930s factories with their pale pink fletton bricks can still be seen on the Estate, but most have been replaced by more modern designs.

Berlie factory. The building was demolished in the 1980s when the firm left Slough, making many workers redundant. In the boom years of the 1950s Berlie offered fringe benefits – such as hairdressing appointments – to attract employees.

Slough Industrial Health Service Recuperative Home at Farnham Park. In 1946 the Slough Estates Ltd, Nuffield Foundation and the Nuffield Provincial Hospital Trust sponsored the Slough Industrial Health Service, the first of its kind in the country to combine industrial health, rehabilitation and research services.

Works rooms provided opportunity for occupational therapy.

Works outing: W.G. Bedford, mechanical engineers, annual outing in 1937.

Brickmakers. The brick earths at Langley were first developed for brickmaking in the 1850s. The largest of the several firms, the Slough and Langley Brickworks, survived into the 1930s until forced to close by the competition from the London Brick Company which produced machine-made bricks. Behind the men are three off-loading barrows for carrying wet bricks to be dried, and a chain-driven pug mill which kneaded the clay mixture to the right consistency for making bricks.

SECTION SIX
Slough's Neighbours

Boveney church, 1858. The tiny village of Boveney lies close to the River Thames, tucked away to the south of Dorney Common. Contrary to what is often said, its church is not in the Domesday Book, although a priest is mentioned. It was built in the twelfth century; the thickness of its walls can be seen in the drawing.

Boveney Lock, 1858. The original lock was a flash lock which dammed up the water and then let it 'flash' through carrying the boat with it over the shallows. This lock was built in 1838 by the Thames Commissioners.

Rebuilding Boveney Lock, 1897. This was one of the first big engineering contracts of Messrs Jackaman of Slough. Jackaman's team of workers are posed in front of the steam-pile driver at the side of the lock.

Burnham Abbey Farm at the turn of the century. The buildings and land belonging to Burnham Abbey were used as a farm from the dissolution of the abbey by Henry VIII until it became an abbey once again in 1912. Mr White was the last tenant farmer.

Threshing with the aid of a steam-engine.

Building the strawstacks. In this part of the country it was usual for haystacks to be rectangular and strawstacks circular.

Dorney: best kept village. Dorney won the award in 1969, and then a special award in 1972. Colonel Philip Palmer of Dorney Court holds the Michaelis Cup.

Dorney village roadsweeper. Born in Cippenham, Lewis Webb worked for forty-seven years for British Rail, taking up roadsweeping in his sixties. He swept and cleaned five miles of parish roads and much of the village's success in the competition was due to his efforts.

White Heather garage, Dorney, *c.* 1922. The filling station and cycle shop was run by Thomas Quartermain; his wife and children are outside the shop. The house was built sometime around 1600.

The restored White Heather house. Thomas Quartermain became very well known for his fine restoration of timber-framed houses. They are often so well done that it is difficult to tell genuine Tudor work from modern alterations and additions.

Taplow village early this century, showing Gurney's grocery and baker's shop in the High Street. Today there are no shops in the village.

Taplow Station Estate, probably in the 1920s.

Taplow Canadian Red Cross Hospital. During the First World War, Lord Astor of Cliveden gave his polo ground for a hospital for the treatment of the Canadian war wounded in Europe.

Visit of the Canadian Mounties in the 1960s. The present buildings were erected during the Second World War by the Canadian Red Cross. For many years it was the National Centre for the Study and Care of Juvenile Rheumatism. Whenever the Canadian Mounties attended the Windsor Horse Show they visited the hospital.

Burnham High Street, *c.* 1910, looking north. Sydney Rhys-Williams' chemist shop is on the right and Hall's butchers on the left.

Burnham Bells parade, *c.* 1950. Here the Cliveden estate's own fire engine is taking part in the annual parade to raise money for the church bells. Before the introduction of the National Health Service such parades were for the local hospitals.

Lent was a small hamlet in Burnham parish connected to the main village by a path. This view looking south down Lent Rise Road across the Thames valley shows its position on one of the river terraces.

Wingrove's Tea Gardens. It was the delight of those that could afford to do so to take tea in the genteel atmosphere of Wingrove's Tea Gardens on the south side of Burham Beeches.

The London General omnibus bringing trippers to Burnham Beeches in the 1920s.

Wingrove's coach park. In the inter-war years Wingrove's adapted to the increased motor traffic by providing a car and coach park. Today the park is the site of Nightingales housing development.

Burnham Beeches donkeys. After the Beeches was bought by the City of London, the area developed as a famous beauty spot. It was used as a place for outings by Londoners, local families and churches from many miles around. The donkeys are thought to have been used for carrying turves (used for fuel, like peat) as well as rides for children.

Celebrations at Farnham Royal early this century. The Farnham Pump no longer graces the centre of the village but has been preserved. The public house, formerly known as the Butchers Arms (just out of sight on the right), has been renamed after it.

Accident at Farnham Common. A fallen tree has crushed the bus.

Stoke Park. This was the new mansion house built for John Penn, the lord of the manor. The main structure was completed by Robert Mason in 1790, but two years later it was redesigned by James Wyatt (of Windsor Castle fame). The gardens were designed by Capability Brown.

West End was one of several small hamlets in the parish of Stoke Poges which, until 1900, stretched to the centre of Slough.

The Crooked Billet today is at Iver Heath, but it is no use searching for records of the original public house in the records of Iver for it stood on the edge of the heath a few hundred yards across the parish boundary, in Langley.

George Green was one of the several villages in Langley parish. It was originally called Westmoor Green, but was renamed after the public house at the Uxbridge Road end of the village. The inn sign can be seen in the photograph.

Bridge Street, Colnbrook looking east towards the bridge. This bridge over the Coln Brook spanned the boundary between Bucks and Middlesex. Its maintenance, with two other bridges, was made the responsibility of the town by the Borough Charter granted to Colnbrook by Henry VIII.

Bridge Street early this century looking west towards the George Inn. In 1904 20 m.p.h. was made the statutory maximum speed, but in built-up areas local authorities authorized a speed limit of only 10 m.p.h.

The Golden Cross Inn, *c.* 1935, was situated on the Bath Road at the western limit of Colnbrook. It was opened in the 1780s and stage wagons regularly stopped there on route to London.

COLNBROOK - BUCKS

PARTICULARS AND CONDITIONS OF SALE OF THE

VALUABLE DE-LICENCED

FREEHOLD PROPERTY

known as

The Old Golden Cross

Bath Road, Colnbrook

Situated on a prominent corner site with the benefit of planning permission in outline for use as a

Petrol Filling Station

VACANT POSSESSION

Sale Catalogue, 1958.

Aerial view of Ditton Park House, 1949. The house and park were bought in 1917 by the Admiralty Compass Observatory. Three years later facilities were made available for experimental work in radio directional finding with Robert Watson-Watts as superintendent of the radio research station. In 1935 the station was responsible for the invention of radar.

The Watson-Watts aerial mast in Ditton Park in 1926. Made of wood, it was 210 ft high; it burnt down the following year.

Cosmopolitan Slough

The Jolly Londoner at its opening about 1960. The first landlords had moved from Edmonton in London and endeavoured to make the residents of Britwell feel at home by creating a London flavour.

Polish children celebrate their Independence Day in 1967.

Members of the Asian Ladies Organization at Orchard School in the early 1980s.

Portrait of Lydia Lattary who was almost certainly the first black lady to work and live in Slough. Sometime before the First World War she was employed as a maid at Spring Cottage, Upton Park. The lady who owns the photograph recalls the pride she experienced when showing Miss Lattary where to shop in Slough.

Lydia Simmons, the first black lady mayor in Slough and the country, being shown work done by the Slough Training Workshop by two Asian students during an open day at the community centre in 1984.

The Church of God of Prophesy at Salt Hill. The church was originally a Church of England chapel, St Michael's mission church, which served the parishes of Farnham Royal and Upton cum Chalvey. In 1973 the chapel was bought by The Church of God of Prophesy Trust, and became a Pentecostal church with a mixed congregation which included people of African, English, Philippine and West Indian origins.

The mayor visits the Hindu temple in Chalvey which was built in 1982. It is only one of several temples and mosques which have added an exotic flavour to the townscape.

The mosque in Uxbridge Road. Children from Wexham Court Middle School visited the mosque when it was being built. The visit was part of a science project studying buildings.

The Welsh church, Capel y Lon, in Stoke Poges Lane was built in about 1946 by members of the Welsh Congregationalists who had come to Slough in great numbers after the development of the Trading Estate. Here services could be conducted in Welsh. In 1982 the chapel was sold; today it is used by the Moslem community and known as Jamia Masjid.

The Welsh Society social evening, 1966. This was the first of a series of musical evenings held at the North Star public house by the Slough and District Welsh Society.

Lieutenant Colonel Assa Singh Johal wearing his war medals beside a picture of himself as a serving officer. He was one of the founder members of the Association of Retired Indian Soldiers formed in Slough in 1984.

Irish football team, early 1960s. Irish people have been working and living in Slough since the mid-nineteenth century, but it was not until 1974 that they acquired their own social club. The football team, known as St Mels, was formed about 1948: it played Gaelic football.

The Scots' Society of St Andrew, Slough and District, was founded in 1933. Here the Society's president is seen addressing the haggis during the Burns Supper and Ceilidh in 1973.

Polish and English Girl Guides march through Slough on their way to St Ethelbert's church in 1962. The Polish Guides can be recognized by their white berets.

Students from Langley language unit with Joan Lestor, MP for Slough and Eton, on a visit to the Houses of Parliament. In 1964 Slough Education Committee began setting up language units to teach children, mainly Asians, for whom English was not their first language.

Changing Fashions

Wedding photographs of three generations of one local family provide an illustration of changing fashions: at Bray in 1890 (above); at Dorney in 1921 (below); at Slough in 1954 (opposite, top).

Sunday best, hats included, was obligatory for these Chalvey residents setting off on an outing in the 1920s.

Window dressing competition: Slough Co-op, 1920s. Today's women can be thankful that the demands of fashion do not mean she has to endure the restrictions of whale-bone corsets.

Dressed for sport, *c*. 1910. F. Hugh Baley of Cippenham Court Farm is ready for a day out with the Slough or Stoke Poges pack of beagles.

Mini skirt competition, 1960. For those who might quibble that such a photograph is not 'historic', the mini skirt will be remembered as the 'costume' of the 1960s.

Acknowledgements

Our thanks are due, above all, to Lesley Hackett of Slough Museum, who gave us so much time and help in selecting and captioning the many photographs that were loaned from the Museum; to Rosemary Madders and Slough Library for the many photographs loaned from the Library; to Marion Scarr for her invaluable comments on the photographs and captions; to the photographers of the *Slough and Windsor Observer* who made available their collection of negatives; and to Peter Ballinger and Terry Brown, from whose collections of postcards and photographs we were allowed to freely select.

We would also like to thank the many other people and organizations who loaned us photographs and prints: Mr Michael Bayley, Mrs Teifi Beynon, Mr Richard Hall, Mr Jaimal Johal, Mr and Mrs Joe Purple, Dr Rattan, Mrs Rosemary Rix, Mr Martin Ryan, Mrs Lydia Simmons, Mr Marian Soroko, Mr Wolf Stephen, Mr and Mrs Ezra Stone, Miss Angela Tuddenham, Mr M. Williams, Mrs Peggy Williams, British Rail, the Department of Medical Photography, Wexham Park Hospital, the Royal Borough Collection (Royal Borough of Windsor and Maidenhead), Slough Borough Council and Thames Water Authority.

We should also like to record our thanks to the many people and organizations who donated photographs to Slough Museum and Slough Library and who gave us permission to reproduce them in this book. The map showing the Trading Estate in 1926 is reproduced with the permission of the Ordnance Survey. Other illustrations were reproduced by permission of the National Pictorial & Press Agency, the *Slough, Windsor & Eton Express* and the *Slough and Windsor Observer*.

Finally, but by no means least, we would like to express our thanks to the many other people who have helped us in our research, in particular Mrs Mary Bentley, Mr Anthony Fanning, Mr Hari Singh Sewak, Mr Mohammed Quraishy and Revd Derek West, and to Jack Neave who kindly rephotographed several photographs for us.